An Insightful Journal for the Spiritual Journey

444

FREEDOM

©2020 by Roni Hopkins
All rights reserved.
ISBN: 978-1-7349035-4-6

JOURNALS OF REALIZATION

"The only truth one could ever die for is the truth they themselves have become"

Roni Hopkins is the creator of *Journals of Realization,* which are a collection of unique journals that specialize in spirituality and consciousness. She has traveled the world, connecting with all walks of life and lives her purpose dedicated to assisting others on their journey. The creation of these journals reflect those experiences and bring a level of universal insight to ones own spiritual path. Journals of Realization encourages you to discover and express your truth, wisdom and ever evolving awareness throughout the pages and beyond them through our virtual discussions.

Every path reveals its truth within you.

www.RoniHopkins.com

PREFACE

Freedom is a state humans have been vying to become on every level in which we find ourselves here on earth. From our identities, beliefs, gender, race, financial, emotional, and physical.

We are constantly seeking to be free in order to truly live.

To seek for a way where we can exist in the liberation of who we are in a world that leaves no room for true freedom in its entirety. We contemplate wanting to be free but are bound to so much of what we are not.

Spiritual Freedom comes from a place that lies within you. It is state in which your spirit lives autonomously without the limitations of anything that would hinder you from your purpose of being. You begin to perceive, process and exist through this realization that you are no longer subjected to the limitations of this world but you transcend them.

It allows you to live from the abundance of eternal consciousness; alleviating all sense of life being anything other than an opportunity to live and explore through it. The spirit flows and guides you through all areas of your life with an assurance that no matter where you find yourself, you will experience it through the pureness of how life was created to be.

Spiritual Freedom is the altruistic nature of the Spirit and all that it is becomes second nature in you.

You are love without having to find it, peace that keeps you in the eye of a storm, joy that is ever flowing, compassion that always leads to understanding, you are forgiveness that sees without judgement, you are the abundance of life that is inexhaustible in giving, you are everything that is forever and you are free to be all that you are and so much more.

This is your Spiritual Journey

From Pen to Paper

Your Thoughts

Your Experiences

Your Realizations

"Freedom lies only in the reality in which life presents to us."

The past is the past. Though our memories remind us of what we once lived, they also bind us to those moments in order for them to remain alive.

Our future is the future. It is in our mind that we try to create what has yet to be revealed and in those possibilities we are bound to what we will never truly know.

In the present moments, when the spirit is showing us exactly what it desires for us to live, it also provides us with everything we need to be fulfilled.

We are free from what was and what has yet to be.

*"See beyond the feelings, Listen Beyond the emotions
There you will find yourself free from them."*

We often think how we feel is the truth of our being. In reality, how we feel is nothing but a response to what we experience.

Not necessarily holding any truth at all

Emotions and feelings can easily become conditioned patterns of responses from old habits, experiences and learned behaviors.

Allow your feelings and emotions to be a door that leads you deeper into understanding your reactions. Seeing and listening beyond them, you will be guided to the truth in which they were created from.

> "*Understanding one another removes you from a state of things being done to you vs things simply being done.*"

The effort of simply trying to understand creates a oneness for you to connect through empathy and love. It will eradicate judgement, victimization, blame and the inability to see ourselves in each other.

It creates a pathway of forgiveness.

We all share in the same human experience but in different ways. When we begin to understand, we get a glimpse of each other hearts and true intentions behind the why.

Storyteller

What is your story?

Begin by saying I have hidden...
The parts you have allowed others to read are just the fictitious
Realities of your imagination and that is just entertainment

A story that is only as good as the one who perceives it, smiles
And gives its' stamp of approval

That is what our values have amounted to. Stamps like
Immigrants traveling through life and gathering approvals to
Enter into a foreign acceptance.

You want to belong but you will never belong because you are
here only for a short while

So take your time to dream a little, become content in the essence
Of being here or there
Find joy in the joy of just simply being human.

What is your story?

Begin by saying I am afraid...
The challenge for you to be seen like black and white movies
Marveled at their ability to create something classic

You being authentic enough to be more than a copy of someone
Else but the entirety of you seen as beautiful works of art
Created by delicate hands and thoughts of perfection

What is your story?

Begin by saying My story is...

Own the very words on each page and let every period embrace
A new sentence

Dare to be all of you all of the time rather than some of you most
Of the time

A divided soul can only live apart for so long before it runs on
Empty

Life is not about roaming around trying to be something,
Anything that tells a good story

But the best stories ever told are the ones that inspired a flame
And ignited a wildfire of dreamers

"Spiritual freedom is not the same as being free."

The evolution of Spiritual freedom does not plateau. It never reaches a point of completion, a point of arrival to a destination that one desires to achieve.

It is never ending.

It is a constant state of experiencing life in ever changing forms and being able to accept whatever form it comes in. The internal drive to want to be fulfilled in all areas of your life is subjected to your ability to flow and accept the ever changing existence of your spirit being free.

One can find themselves free one moment and bound to that very freedom in the next. As we hold on to a former state of being that the spirit has evolved us through.

"Seize to pay attention to thoughts that do not speak your truth."

Thoughts demand attention and the more you give into them, the more they desperately need your recognition.

Deeply breathe until you find your truth at the center of each breath, then deeply let all of your thoughts go.

As the Spirit creates a state of freedom where thoughts no longer control your mind but are mastered by your eternal nature of absolute existence. Your truths will naturally speak louder the more you begin to listen to them.

> "All that you protect yourself from are the parts of you that need to be set free."

You can become a prisoner to your own protection from life and never realize that you hold the key to the very thing you are protecting yourself from.

We create these boundaries from the experiences that we fear will repeat or experiences that we fear will become our reality. Our human nature protects us as a natural aid to endure life.

The space of vulnerability, without the boundaries, when applied in the purest state of letting go, it is then, when All of your existence is truly set free.

The Spirit is not bound by the hurt of the past or the fear of a future.

It is part of the spiritual journey to become aware of oneness through vulnerability and letting go. A surrender of all that you fear, for all that you are completely free from.

"Not having control does not imply things are out of control."

The awareness of not having control does not imply things are out of control or that they need to be controlled at all. Life is simply offering you freedom from carrying the responsibility of the situation and the opportunity to see the natural flow of life constantly working on your behalf.

Only in this position can you experience the fullness of life creating life though you and for you. It is an effortless flow that you will discover the spirit's ability to create perfection.

I promise.

Catch a moment before time flies
And you fly with it

From city to city and through the oceans expanse
We are flying in between the freedom of life that was before us
and the life that is ahead

For forever is a long time
And I promise that I can give it to you
Though it has no end in sight

But I see

You gazing upon my horizon
Witnessing what you once believed

Creating love that is endless

This is how I remember our moments
As time flies and we have found ourselves flowing in Freedom
The memories that hold the remembrance of you and I

The forever and always

It was inevitable for nothing to remain the same
And I often wondered if I could change its mind

Just this one time

For forever is what I promised you
And Love is the forever that remains

> "*Deeply find Joy in the freedom of letting Go vs the heartache of trying to hold on.*"

Freedom lies in the letting go and that often leads us to heartache and holding on to moments of life that we can never have again.

In the goodbyes, the memories begin to take on a life in our present reality, replaying moments that no longer exist and longing to give life to something that no longer lives.

Life is ever flowing into new memories that evolve from the old ones.

Spiritual freedom releases moments like dandelions escaping in the wind, constantly creating new life wherever they land. If we can embrace the joy in the letting go, then we will find ourselves free to live life once more.

" The Spirit uses freedom as the canvas to create the possibilities of your life."

Outside of what you can create, what your mind can dream into physical reality, lies the spirit and it's passion of artistry of using your life as its canvas.

It desires for you to experience your life through all facets of freedom. For your spirit knows no other way to be.

It takes what you can dream simply as the foundation and from there, it creates all your desires into a reality without any limitations to what you can experience from them.

The dreams that we envision for ourselves are only the prelude to the possibilities of our spirits creativity.

"Life is Eternally being Free."

Spiritual Freedom is a flow of life that is eternally presenting us with new ways to experience. As life continues to live through you, this beautiful point of existence becomes your solace, your hope and the truest of desires that guides you through every chapter of your life.

We were created to live in the abundance of what we are and when we begin to understand what that is, our lives surpass all obstacles and limitations for us to freely be it.

It is the Spirits destiny for us to live eternally Free.